Cards on the Table

Jeremy Roberts

Interactive Press

Interactive Press
an imprint of IP (Interactive Publications Pty Ltd)
Treetop Studio • 9 Kuhler Court
Carindale, Queensland, Australia 4152
sales@ipoz.biz
ipoz.biz/IP/IP.htm

First published by IP in 2015

Printed in 12 pt Cochin on 14 pt Avenir Book.

National Library of Australia
Cataloguing-in-Publication entry:

Creator:	Roberts, Jeremy N., author.
Title:	Cards on the table / Jeremy Roberts.
ISBN:	9781925231113 (paperback)
Subjects:	Poetry--21st century.
	New Zealand poetry--21st century.
Dewey Number:	NZ821.4

to Eden

Acknowledgements

Book design: David P. Reiter

Cover image: Ben Livingston, "Forever Stamp"

Author photo: Brian DiPierdomenico

Grateful acknowledgement is made to the editors & publishers of magazines & journals where some of this work previously appeared: *Side Stream, Live Lines, Poetry NZ, JAAM, Free Venice Beachhead* (California) *Takahe Magazine, NZ Listener, Snorkel, Potroast,* NZ Poetry Society's *"a fine line", "the years hold hands" anthology, Frankfurt Bookfair 2012: An Aotearoa Affair, Blackmail Press, Phantom Billstickers, Jakarta Expat* (Indonesia), *Poetry 24, Debris, Landfall.*

A big gracias must be given to many friends & colleagues who have given support & inspiration – the Auckland Poetry Live 'family' – especially Penny Somervaille, Rachael Naomi, Tim Heath, Makyla Curtis, Michelle Bolton, Miriam Larsen-Barr, & Kiri Piahana-Wong; event organisers – especially Ila Selwyn, Gus Simonovic, Siobhan Harvey, Michelle Leggott, Anita Arlov, Ron Riddell, Nigel Gavin, Michelle Elvy; others who come to mind – Cathie Dunsford, Terry Sturm, Nicholas Reid, Owen Bullock, Michael Morrisey, Lizzy Gardner, Mark Leaning, Nick Wade, Jay Burrows, Linde Walker, Jane Gardner, James Alcock-Roberts, Kevin Stewart, Darren Shrek, Rocky Terita, Angie Tidy, & other NZIS staff.

A debt of gratitude also to the musicians who have played with me to date & enhanced my poetry: Rasam Moghimi, Derek Fraser, Dan Kaplan, Ardiansyah Erwin, Bambang Ferdian, Michael Walsh, Aaron Longville, Nigel Gavin, Paul Williams, Chris Andrews, Red Lamp Auckestra, & Eden Spence.

Contents

CARDS ON THE TABLE

is a staircase more
useful than a ladder?

is turquoise prettier
than blue?

is a knife more decisive
than an axe?

a cloudy sky has
a different meaning
from a clear one.

such as? You might ask.
well, it's your life –
& you must decide.

BREATHING TRICK

the siege engine will carry us thru, like all those before.
it was built in God's own auto shop / breaks the speed of light.

where we're going, fear is surely a mere hat –
blown from a head;
human philosophy a shit argument.

anger? only a worm under a hot blue sky –
while these auras of inevitability will soon be glowing
like Hiroshima!

when that last coffee is finished, we'll leave the others
slumped with burden, or happy as hell –
still gasping.

the sparrows are coming with us because every
cliché is about to die.

beauty will break apart completely;
inquiry will not exist.

we are going thru the wall of time.

PERMANENTLY TEMPORARY

for Jay

it seems to me now –
looking back,
how temporary everything
really was.

I watched a flake of concrete
fall off a verdigris-laden wall,
& flutter to the ground.

it was now part of
the ground – no longer
part of the wall.

what is there to fear?
not being able to hold on?

it is our destiny
to eventually tumble from each apogee,
to slip off the ledge
          & crash
however softly, through the branches
of the very trees
                  we grew!

landing
          where
                  we
                      must.

it's okay.
this is merely
how the game is played.

THE FREAKS OF VENICE

the roar of the jets
is the roar of the ocean –
& that's all you need to know about
God's plan.

the freaks of Venice Beach
meant to write that down & sell it
in day glow paint –
but they're too busy, being freaks

chewing the scenery – with the status of
movie-stars, who never sold out,
spewing confessional sound bites

which bounce off cruising black & whites
& slide all over the body of tattooed Marilyn –
who leans against walls, everywhere
in assured, iconic empathy.

ah – their screams:
drunk, stoned
or straight as an arrow

they snuggle neatly around that lizard tongue
which still licks Ocean Front Walk
clean of irony.

Here, You Know Where You Are & What You Know

as you wander around
feasting on coffee & cinnamon rolls;

digging:

that Chuck Norris only ever has two speeds –
walk & kill;

how forty bucks can get you a 'legal marijuana'
certificate;

observations of kinetic malfunction
at Muscle Beach – are free;

& the beachfront apartment sign that says
I can make it to the fence in 1.5 seconds – Can you?
is not a joke.

it's while you're checking out t-shirts of the dead &
spectacularly over-rewarded
you realise fame just might sink into the sea
here at Venice –

leaving fundamental humanity.

but we'll still have the freaks –
who always have their shit together –
even when they haven't.

even though their humanity is
a pure karmatic truth of often haunting
pictures –

psycho-derelict shadows, sparkling filth
& shifting registrations
etched deeply into the lens…

they understand that

Everything in Your Life Led to Where You Are Now

& when they're tired? they just lie down
a little bit harder than most
on the concrete pillows of a system they are deeply
rooted in.

the freaks of Venice:
life-splattered players & jittery receptors
playing out their moment, by the waves

beneath that year-round Los Angeles sun
as if it was some divine beach ball – set on fire
& kicked into the sky –

& because they know
the Pacific Ocean has already
swallowed them all.

AT THE TACO EXPRESS

at the Taco Express down on Lamar
Che Guevara stares from a wall –

watching a couple struggle
with a crossword puzzle.

the woman – I've seen an hour before,
browsing in a sex shop.
the man she's with is focused on something
not in the room.

above the bar is a yellow plastic sun with a clock face,
hands stopped – probably for years

& we're fine with that, because in the beer-sign light
you can read the paper & drink a $3.50 Margarita
on a Monday morning –

tapping out a little dance with your fingers on the table top,
quietly pondering normal stuff:

how damn near the same all our lives are;

the hairy notion of bonding with something in the ether;

whether it's time for a personal revolution –
if you could actually pull it off.

CLEAR THINKING THRU A CAFÉ WINDOW

the way thought bubbles float away on Kitchener St
is part of the order of the world:

everything booked in; ready to leave.
the trick – to let it *all* go.

even that Pompeii heart.
sometimes, the deeper you go, the bullet you are.

but it's ok – pulling the trigger,
or taking the hit;

waiting for the rubbish collection –
your body an alien theme-park ride of strange delights…
working out all the shit, as the punctured ego
heals –

slowly getting a handle on a better here & now,
chilling your ass in cafés like this one:

drinking an ocean of extra-strong coffee
& riding the angle of that caffeine gradient…
ticking off, thru the window:

how well the strike of the clock
& bounces of breasts work together;

as do tattoos on hoboes;

& that pneumatic pigeon gait – perfectly in time with
"Highway to Hell"…

& quietly pondering again –
Euphemia's interesting question beside the stacked-up
dishwasher in the restaurant kitchen,
thirty years before:
"Do you think life is too easy?"

TUATARA BITES INTRUDER & LAUGHS!
or
WHY IS OUR NATIONAL SYMBOL A FLIGHTLESS BIRD?

once upon a ponga log…

an old tuatara sat, in native bush beside a stream flowing through Maori, Crown, private land. he loved to bask in the early sun, flicking through memories of colonial war & ink, the whistling of Hone Heke's axe fiercely displacing air, the brutal stripping of the land, the Suffragettes, All Black victories, Billy T's jokes, the legendary 'swappa-crate', the price of milk…

the story of a nation.

this morning, a fresh roar from distant towns & cities was in the air, disrupting his peace. headlines were clattering loudly with some new obsession & the tuatara chuckled his famous leathery chuckle…

what the hell was going to fall out of the long white cloud this time?

weak justice? strange, annoying new migrants? unfair taxes? yet another politician pissing in his own pocket? was paradise about to be lost? the worry was unbearable!

after not moving for what seemed an age, the tuatara spoke.

'Yes, this paradise, this home – *has* been through a lot. & fast! You'd think Maui's ropes had snapped!' he giggled. 'There's been good shit, bad shit. There's been bad shit come out of good shit, good shit come out of bad shit. & a fair bit of bullshit!

What the hell…I wasn't chosen as the national symbol – they chose that blind, flightless bird – but I didn't vanish like some tourist drowned in a turquoise riptide, either!'

he giggled again & for another long time sat very still, staring into the future…

'Aotearoa will survive!' he finally said, humming the old Gloria Gaynor hit & sucking on a few mls of spider juice…

the tuatara looked up through the sky, far beyond the noise being made by the lobbyists, the committees, the media, & all manner of holy defenders – howling yet again, wringing their hands in disbelief at the prospect of their nation changing beyond recognition.

he winked at speed freak Ra – who was busy as usual, lighting & heating the landscape, rolling out the seasons –

& yawned the words:

'New Zealand – open your transition mouth a little wider, & receive what is coming!'

INVITATIONS FROM UNKNOWN PLACES

that ill, hazy light of non-engagement
is back.

when you're a little down *(fill in the appropriate reason)*
& haven't spoken to anyone for several days
the mind slips into another place -
shadowless & flat
& gets messed-up in solipsistic ways.

time begins to move sideways
                              & the distance ahead disappears
in a blinding
white-out of emotional optics.

suddenly you realise that your hands are completely free
but that the criterion was secretly growing –
until it had pushed
right through the ceiling of the room
you'd painted yourself into
                                    in horrible, crippled colours.

how often do we see – absolutely, what we want
right in front of us?
we want to, though –

to avoid
that slow crawl across the vast space:
chasing the voices, gestures, energies...

pages & pages of blueprints
blowing across the surface

of the world.

THE TREE OUTSIDE MY WINDOW

for Owen Bullock

the temporary tree outside my window is bending –
furiously, in the wind; anchored.

it's a class act.
wind is a free-ranging show pony – lacking finesse at
times:

unable, say – to slip exclusively thru portals,
tending to fly straight into anything it approaches

but forever regulating power, changing direction.
I'm envious –

floating in the pool, watching lightning overhead –
stuck on how much we gaze.

an intense outflow of electricity in the air – occurring within
clouds, among clouds, or between a cloud & the surface of the
earth

relentless precision, interaction –
an exploding nest of verbs!

my behaviour?
not so tree-like.

freeze-frames of choosing & tasting –
the details of which are ultimately lost in summation:

an existence –
somewhere between waiting in line

& riding the tick-tock click track up to the final
roaring descent.

LIFE, FOR DUMMIES

it can now be revealed!

the first half
is a kind of
Analytical Cubism.
(taking things apart).

the second half
is a kind of
Synthetic Cubism.
(putting things back together).

enough penetration?

nothing like
a one-person commission
of inquiry, into the burning

    QUESTION.

a self-given Ink-Blot test,
            seeking clues –
reconnaissance into

    LIFE:

scratching around
        on the intricate surface …
as the second cup
of coffee
    kicks in –
        on another spectacularly elusive,
reassuringly ordinary,

        idiot afternoon.

BOMB THE POETRY FACTORIES

l
lo
loo
look
look h
look he
look hea
look hear
look hear s
look hear sm
look hear sme
look hear smel
look hear smell
look hear smell t
look hear smell to
look hear smell tou
look hear smell touc
look hear smell touch
look hear smell touch t
look hear smell touch ta
look hear smell touch tas
look hear smell touch tast
look hear smell touch taste
write it down

A BALCONY IN INDONESIA

for Derek

sipping vodka with Trotsky in old Batavia…

watching mosquito aerobatics on a thermal
transfiguration skyline:
dive-bombing sleeping bodies on a building site below!

the fine art of extracting blood –
blood rising on wings!

we drink to the future,
the murdered Communists of '65,
& the cries of goats the day before they meet the knife.

in daylight there are several glass towers of luxury,
a green lawn & the glimpse of a swimming pool.
drivers wash & polish cars, smoke & mutter about the boss…

'Ah, the struggle…' Trotsky chuckles. 'Life is not an easy
matter. You can keep the poor happy with cheap petrol
& cheap cigarettes…for a while.'

right on cue – distant thunder.
'The elements,' he observes –

'Beware ideas that enter the mind under fire.'

REASONS (The Vortex of Violence)

I know these streets like the back of the hand that frequently slapped me across the face, with Thelonius Monk-like syncopation. (Oh yeah, I know my music.)

my brain is wired differently to yours. I'm trained to listen to the tone of voices, to watch feet & hands very closely & to be aware of sudden movements.

I'm programmed for flight, Jack. I do what I have to do & get out.

I know the sound of running footsteps, believe me.

I'm always ready to hit the highway & the highway usually hits back.

when I was kicked, I crawled across the hard, wooden floor – my nails digging into the timber – towards the high window in the house where we lived.

it was actually perfect for swan-diving into anger's improvised theatre & alcohol's warm, electric bonfire.

you can call me an outsider, but at least I'm free. I watch the carloads, busloads, & truckloads of home dwellers sprint by – the crush & the rush.

society flakes with a hoard of dreams, clutter & aspirations that are all foreign to me. tea-drinking society members living in mini-museums, stuffed with baubles – all with serious emotional cost.

I'm the filth that walks. I'm the spew outside a bar. I'm the reason you want your kids to get a good education. I'm the shit that flows through the back alleys. I walk on the cracks. I steal sugar from cafés & I scorch police cars with my eyes.

PROTOTYPE

if you accept Andy Warhol's vision
you need never go into an art gallery again.

just walk down the street or supermarket aisle
& check out the visual feast:
brands, signs, labels, logos.
read a newspaper – but focus on the
pictures, headlines & ads.

art no longer had to come from
an artist's private angst
or carry an important message.
the beauty in good design was suddenly
noticed & accepted.

some would also argue that he was an
out-there, crazy motherfucker –
constantly asking to photograph men's cocks
& having once been shot nearly dead by some crazy bitch –
stating that he liked guns & that they were rather
nice.

in fact, Andy Warhol's vision was truly
a revolution.
he taught us to accept the ordinary, love the bland
& see depth in the superficial.
all it needed was a veneer of glamour.

& now he is a god –
projecting his movies from the void
where everything comes from
& where everything returns.

ABANDONED BUILDING SITE NOTES

hole in ground
pond of brown water for happy birds
found image of toetoe sparklers-in-the-wind!
chain-link fence begs to be jumped
spray paint yells at capitalism

– imagining Tai Chi on the tips of rusted, metal rods
– thinking of those vanished tonnes of dirt

I feel an air of revolution…
when will I rupture in God's fingers like a Chinese
cookie?

SHE NEVER KNEW

he was only going to write a few buildings
jump off a few poems –

content, in late-night exile
but ended up walking that hard-edged
freezing drunken mile of tongue-rolling bullshit again –
a poisoned happy valley in his back pocket

all because he saw a woman whose hand-gestures
played wind-chime notes.

she was probably capable of holding
the Milky Way in her head
while grinding misguided souls to dust
with a screeching laugh

but he was hooked on her ability
to transport herself into his day.

he wanted to run after her scent
through the moonlit Biboli Gardens in Florence
among the wild, starving felines who live there

or travel with her on a boat, to visit Maat –
the Egyptian god of truth.

she never knew how cold it was
frequently chewing ice-cubes from the bottom
of his glass – pondering the skeleton inside each of
her words.

she never knew how ravishing the deception felt; how
spectacular the glimmer.

let's just say it was the tilt of the Earth's axis:
the universe showing off – beaming holograms
of undelivered sanctuary
& pleasure

making him fall backwards through symbolic rain
hoping *she* would catch him.

REFLEX

what did you think your life was going to be like
on these old roads –

with second-hand information,
limited skills & only so many miracles
to go around?

& time –
thundering like an angry, virus-spitting bull –
running hard at you, in your own doorway?

& what of Cezanne's thing?
everything in nature reduced to a cylinder, sphere
or cone?

you've done pretty well relating to those shapes,
squinting thru the alphanumeric confusion

& dealing with all the famous metaphors…
including the ultimate "thousand-yard stare".

how are you supposed to react to such mystery?

laugh?
mistakes probably won't matter

when the world becomes colourless, the wind visible
& the light – solid in your hands,

as you pull yourself away
from the world.

THE MIRROR

Picasso claimed he could stare into the sun.

how good are you at polishing
your own bullshit?

WINTER MOMENT

a morning power-saw in weak sun – loud!
& in charge.

to cut moments to pieces like that!

or be
one of the laughing sparrows –
translating themselves sideways, in quick notation

with glances as cognizant as the world
ever is.

it's another role to hover
on astro-turf –

replicating inquiry, in the grip of a
reflex

beneath a chilly blue promise of
nothing – which is the mortar;

our actions – the colouring-in
of all those gaps –

the mind pondering
choices...

seeking warm, solid
reality.

TOPLEXIL SLEEP MEDICATION KICKS IN

Hey Hanoi – I'm coming to you
I'm climbing aboard the B52
Was only a kid when the bombs were falling
Ho Chi Minh & the States were brawling

cough! swallow – waiting for impulse to lessen...mental list fading, pattern on bed cover emerging: repeating rectangles grey & burgundy – view from plane window: crops & fields / blood & old skin – a board game of plastic Bazookas & tiny soldiers.

all's fair in love & war, mother said & the pillow a soft atom cloud for my head – how much time did Albert Einstein spend in bed? he hated the A – Bomb. I'm dropping now... battle of the day over, but only battle of *Western* man in reasonable luxury.

Pete Townshend wrote: *I've known no war* – but so many families have & tick tick tick says the clock. what time do I leave for airport?

have to remember: shampoo & conditioner...transfer from big container to little, otherwise I possible danger? dangerous as landmine?

reading: post-war landmine dead or wounded in Vietnam: 100,000 / Agent Orange: generations of horrific genetic distortion. travel articles say 'landscape has healed', yet teams of mine-clearing still in operation & suffering mutants people wouldn't believe.

I curl my toes & stretch my limbs...

not everybody gets that innocent world I had as a boy – waking in pure light, wide-eyed... & the smell of everything! certainly not napalm in the morning & never terror in the rain outside – beyond the curtain: burning children running down the road. but they were out there – just a little further from sleepy eyes.

photo-man Tim Page declared: *You can't take the glamour out of war* & he was there with shrapnel in the brain...

what can you do when the enemy is coming to do you ill? Look good as you run up the hill, engaging deadly machinery. helicopters thunder overhead as politicians discuss numbers of dead over lunch, dinner – fingers all over the menu. just keep those body-bags off TV! – unless we're winning, because *war is an extension of politics* & good business. the job of government: make the agenda a just cause & only admit years later, it was wrong. it's fun being a cock. It's fun being a cunt. It's fun being an asshole. & it's an old bedtime story: Vietnam – plenty of blood, screams, exploding body parts, politicians neck-deep in atrocity – & also true: when you're President, you're allowed to murder...

Nixon was never a friend of mine
But I loved his evil smirk
They say he died & went to Hell
& now hustles in the dirt

THE GUARD

I know that guard sitting in his uniform in the hot bright sun,
guarding something

is a guard sitting in his uniform
in the hot bright sun.

the day might be hanging by a thread, but that guard is
there –
guarding, for all he's worth.

his head turns as I laugh out loud, offering me a slight nod.
'Hail team spirit!' I mutter quietly,

walking away thru the steamy air; the shuddering
sounds of traffic & birds fading in & out –

happy, in our fellowship of
uncertainty.

PROTEST HOWEVER YOU WANT, BUT DO NOT GO ONTO THE STREETS & SQUARES

thursday morning @ 6.39 was looking every bit like a wet,
mediocre canvas.
a surface to be discarded, burned
or terrorised.

I would have counted the dots of rain on the window
or the number of cars surging up my hill –
just so many scuttling silverfish, under contract to
The Man.
money really was standing up & shouting:
'Who's your 1st religion, cog-man?'

I was feeling that ordinary!

my sacred coffee ritual failed to hit the target
& I felt like seizing the earth in both hands
& stopping the spin.
or at least – kicking the damn coffee pot
& starting again,
but I ironed my pants & shirt, like a good boy
& prepared to go to work.

there *were* a couple of compensatory highlights:
Tom Waits talking about Keith Richards
& my daughter's request to hear Charlie Parker
on the stereo.

9 o'clock was a room full of school children –
a slowly melting, wobbly jelly
reuniting in crayon & dye.

I gave them my all.

at 3pm I flipped the switch
& felt the need to do something offensive.

you know: *Fuck Shit Up!*

in my mind, I said:
give me a good shot of tequila
& a weapon
& some originator of irritation is going to die!

at the very least, I felt like drilling a hole in the head of Gaddafi.

instead, there was a brief, café experience
which was mostly tit-gazing & overheard wedding plans
beneath fading, old photos of Turkey...

& through the front door
the noisy, sideways parabola of a yellow motorcycle.
but he didn't lose it, or slide into a wall!
he rode carefully & made sure he got home.

& a lame, computer-enhanced pop vocal
blasting through a car window – which was just too much of a Gaga moment to bear.
so I wished the singer & fan, intense ill.

at least my coffee –
my compromising, mind balm was served hot!
& with a nice, bitter aftertaste.

I finished that, over a few casual thoughts
about how you would justify 4thGenerationWarfare.

IS ALL RAIN THE SAME?

God taking a piss?

Rangi crying for Papatuanuku?

is it controlled by Queen Madjadji of South Africa?

or Yinglong, the Chinese Maker of Rain?

maybe all you need is a Native American Indian rain stick?

is it really just the farmer's friend?

fuck off.
rain is rain.

SURF NAZIS

watching the 1987 trash movie classic *Surf Nazis Must Die* –
about a gang of sick bullies in California,
a glorious wave of politically incorrect fantasy shot thru me.
I was feeling as happy as a Jew on the day Hitler shot
himself!

how could I use this gift?
I remembered a friend of mine back in '83, taking a shit
on the bonnet of a CEO's car – which I didn't fancy
doing myself –
but it did lead me to consider how victims feel.

I remembered laughing & teasing a boy at school one day –
for the crime of 'looking like an ugly warthog'.
a friend & I teased the crap out of this kid,
reducing him to tears, chanting 'Warthog! Warthog!'

we thought it was so funny – in a vicious, thrilling kind
of way.
what do I remember most?
the look on his face – the hurt & disbelief.
the world was picking on us, so we picked back.

we enjoyed our roles that day.
we were innocent little fools – stuck in our ugly,
frustrated adolescence.
trapped in the cruel school playground, we were itching
to do anything that might release us.

it all came back so clearly
& a feeling of shame swept thru me – so many years
later.
I decided to do nothing –
even though the world loves a victim.

WAY TO GO

'I'll just pop off, one of these days,' my grandmother told us
& the old leaf did suddenly let go.

singer Warren Zevon knew *he* was going to die
& wrote a song after the news – "My Ride's Here".

& then, the jumpers from the twin towers –
falling thru death-chamber blue
one fine September morning –

exploding like water bombs
on the concrete below.

BEAUTIFUL RUBBISH

I love you, dear artefact
of a time & place straining for higher knowledge
& reasons.

your purpose is over –
a mere plastic wrapper, floating up from the Thames
& easily defined:

part of all the shit we create – yet also
complete.

we're the *living* product
of modern, sophisticated factories

& are also ripped open; used
twisted & crushed
squeezed dry

blown from the river.

little leaves dipped in fake gold
supposed to disappear
& we do –

back into the jackpot of volition.

let's cling to the belief
that there is vision in demolition, destruction
& decay.

let's cling to the hope that life has always rhymed
with *mysterious* – for good reason

& there are no more labels when the dots are all joined
by whatever it is – that pushes the button.

let that wind take us.

COMFORTING PHRASES

the flow of life is not
disturbed

by pretending we're
dogs licking shit off the sidewalk

or pieces of gum on the soles of shoes –
hidden from the world.

& if imaginary fat girls dance naked on car bonnets
because we've watched *Blue Velvet* too many times,

let them shake it!
when the world is dull, the mind *will* wander –

as you wait for T-Rex to come & suck the eyeballs
out of your skull.

a world of brutal nails –
hammered home, regardless.

BOLD MOVES AGAINST CONVENTIONAL PERSPECTIVE

apparently, when it rains
thousands of people write poems
called "Rain."

raindrops are commas, falling from the sky
& in between – bionic neon
shines thru the icy hail
like severed entrails from Heaven.

it was a wet day,
when I fell in love with Frances Farmer –

among fading, blond follicles of sun
                    in an autumn embroilment of youthful
                                        confusion

& twisting lambs wool scarves.

I loved her
anger
battles with Hollywood
struggles with self
rebellious nature

her *bold moves against conventional perspective*.

watching such a precious living thing
                                                            push
against the current
& go under
was so utterly seductive
when I was apparently choosing failure.

'You've got to take stock of your life!' they said,
as if I preferred brutal, cartoon versions of the world.

they didn't understand that
depression

is sometimes unavoidable
& can be like the most potent, hypnotic perfume
carried by the breeze
to the frail house in your head.

I wanted Frances & I
to create our own, earthy counterpoint
against their bland, sanctioned melancholia
& rules.

instead of two battered leaves
floating on disturbed waters
eventually going down the drain –

we'd see ourselves as
two white yachts on a calm blue sea

suddenly standing up & walking off together.

CLOWNS

I grew up without realising
that many people fear clowns.

I always liked how they
present the idea of hiding
from the world, but being able
to interact with people,
while wearing a mask of make-up
& a costume.

kind of like your average Human.

CAFÉ LIST

trace of cigarette smoke

vague communal feeling: *Well, here we are*

round table smeared with bird shit

order dark roast coffee; chocolate brownie w/ whipped cream

free water; free *Redbull* magazine

check out that set-piece worker precision-ordering!

the sound that Ferrari made was exactly like a wild animal!

business man asks a colleague: 'How's *your* stream flowing?'

art student subtext: 'How are *we* going to make it?'

plumber in from London says: 'I got your number in the *yellow* pages'

Marvin Gaye sings "Sexual Healing"

thru the window, a road sign: *HAZARD*

Ian Curtis sings "Love Will Tear Us Apart"

so many forgotten, irretrievable fantasies

memory of a dark-haired, complicated, irritating girl

gone somewhere

where is *The Wild Blue Yonder*?

the left & right side of my brain form a détente, while the ocean pours from my mouth

Jim's description: *peristaltic rhythm*

I never did heroin, never went to 'Nam, never joined the Ku Klux Klan

Pet Shop Boys sing about making lots of money

are those sparrows in here, wearing leather?

why are animals in here?

travel back to that kiss

it only became a mystery, afterwards

favourite palindrome: 1991

favourite palindrome #2: *murder for a jar of red rum*

what are we doing besides eating panini & smiling at each other thru cyberspace?

fuck cyberspace!

fuck face & return to the mountain

toilet here is filthy

write *give me a quick history of your love* in pencil, on the wall

why can't I meet anyone?

I wish I was a fighter pilot

leave with a half-empty stomach, following pink wool hovering above black tights

the needle of the sky tower is the needle of the universe & is sticking in my mind

THE PUNK M.O.

don't blindly accept the products &
instructions issued by corporations
& governments.

D-I-Y

Carbon Footprint?

shit, that expression pisses me off!

you know –
the jet-setting big-shots
getting together to tell us
how to live.

where can I get a bucket of that goddamn carbon,
so I can think Globally,
act Locally,
& shove it down some
politician's vote-grabbing
cake-hole …

you know what I mean.

IN HANOI BEFORE

I've never taken that long, curious taxi ride from
airport – in Hanoi before; never greeted strangers with
optimism – in Hanoi before; never woken suddenly late
afternoon, lifted head from pillow & wondered what the
time was – in Hanoi before; never sat at the breakfast
table, staring into space, thinking about nothing –
in Hanoi before; never realised it is all nothing – in
Hanoi before; never checked the state of my nasal hair,
itched my balls – in Hanoi before; never not read the
newspapers – in Hanoi before; never peered into my
wallet & calculated cash – in Hanoi before; never stared
into the sky & felt that weird cosmic unease – in Hanoi
before; never glanced at my watch & felt the trick of
time – in Hanoi before; never smelt the waft of cigarette
smoke & been reminded of my grandfather's white-out
haze – in Hanoi before; never been proud of myself for
abandoning alcohol – in Hanoi before; never been talked
into sucking on communal spliff & been disappointed
at how weak the weed was – in Hanoi before; never
heard Louis Armstrong sing *Wonderful World* – in Hanoi
before; never felt content being on my own – in Hanoi
before; never consumed 3am coffee & biscuits – in Hanoi
before; never watched *FASHION TV* – in Hanoi before;
never been liked by Facebook friends – in Hanoi before;
never lain on the bed, nestling my skull in the crook of
my elbow – in Hanoi before; never gazed across morning
rooftops, feeling bird envy – in Hanoi before; never
felt sun warming skin & memories – in Hanoi before;
never walked streets - full of 20,000 & some days, heart
beating, eyes still seeking - in Hanoi before.

CANVAS

we're all seekers,
choosing a bit / living a bit –

sometimes, our gestures like hungry
painters…

it was only a quick sketch
of you –
in that rain of light:

walking down the hill in a glow of burnt umber
& greenish yellow –

pure Vincent, really.

how would *he* deal with you?
a woman from Holland –

his eyes in such focus?
Vincent eyes

they were mine,
as you leaned back against a lime wall –

all starry, swirling
possibilities…

I'VE ALREADY HAD FOREVER

majestically unattached to anything –

the sky seemed always
above

rather than passing thru us

which is the harder, swallowed truth
of memory.

the sky is a street

of fading photos & distant audio recordings…
a collection of smashed skulls

falling
on the roof of every moment.

inside
the pages stack like an ephemeral manuscript
that can't be saved

about
school children who left sandwiches to dry in the sun
the once crystal-clear chirping of birds
the mental fists & sweet farts of adolescent
defiance…

thru the light-fingered moments of a love career
wearing that huge, dripping grin in the bedroom…

& all the scenes
where there was only was a sliver of face on broken
mirror, a doom-ticket in back pocket.
it's all there!

& between every page, pressed flat
lie a million inspirations – now ghostly dust.

still –
what's coming round that polished corner?

what's left, besides the phone call to the CEO?
& just holding a steady watch on the remaining eras –

wearing that pigmentation of feeling
thru this eerie, hand-written world –

pouring out breath & decisions into the great sky
of evaporation?

CHERRY BRANDY & THE LEAP OF FAITH

I dreamt I saw
a bottle of cherry brandy on a shelf, high in the clouds –
next to a tired-looking Jesus
& a group of nasty-looking angels, who were
smoking dope & reading cum-covered porno mags…

there was a billboard in the sky
behind them, that said in giant letters:
YEAH?
(& in little letters underneath)
That's right – we need to fuck off, too!

it was a vivid dream.
I think it was one of those referred *Wizard of Oz* moments.

I still wanted to taste cherry brandy.
I still wanted to know how things were hanging in Heaven.

CONNECTION

the view from the chopper –
children scattering in an Asian schoolyard

is as vivid as napalm.
that banana could be the sixties, too – a famous LP cover

except it's brown & rotting in the sun.
children never stay young

& white light splits apart
into feedback & darkness.

Lou Reed won't need his morning coffee anymore
& he won't be waiting for the man –

because he's not waiting for the man
anymore.

even though he walked past me today
on a street in Jakarta.

CYANIDE LOVE

the fear of loss & giddy
reality of arrival – unavoidable!

your stormy, dark fuss of hair
& stinging forecasts

finally blew themselves out –
& disappeared…

leaving only
the squeak of my hindsightful pen.

it felt as if we'd lived for centuries,
but it was always a feeble hope:

looking back together.
we'd already walked our ancient gardens.

we were left with footnote phone calls;
mental loops with broken sprockets –

damaged by poor light
& sad, persistent unease…

it was always a jingle-jangle morning
of failing props, & glass reflections

of a cyanide love:
it had to die.

'Too bad – we look so good together,' I said.

they named a dance after us:
Do the Cyanide – heard in every club in town.

each time felt like you – screaming in my face:
'The dance you only do once!'

& we had – among the Russians, remember?
your warm syrup still on my face,

& Solzhenitsyn saying how good it felt
to be free.

DESTINATIONS

I'm sure the smirk in that irreverent wind
is exactly as it was
the time I walked through the backstreets of Charleville
hunting Arthur's ghost.

at 23
I stood in front of his rain-flecked, immaculate grave
muttering thanks – for synthesizing pain
into longed-for spectrums of exhilaration
& showing how poets can die
twice.

I ambled respectfully beside the river Muse
which he probably pissed into –
convinced of some delectable, poisonous influence
hidden within.

I studied his rudimentary possessions
through expensive museum glass – convinced they were fake
& was shocked to see his image on coffee mugs.

I stared at one of his childhood houses
speculating about his mother's love for her possessed son.

I didn't get nearly drunk & disorderly enough – in the
old, tatty bars he frequented.

I had my photo taken beside a memorial bust
by a Japanese fan, who proudly showed me his translation
of *Illuminations*.

we were all so in awe of this little French kid
who'd no idea he would live in so many hungry,
unsatisfied young minds.

when it was time to leave, I waited for six hours
for a train to Paris, speaking to no one in an empty
railway station –
disappointed I could hardly write a line.

so much for fucking a French girl in the town
& being shot dead by her father…

so much for slipping into madness…

I just got on that train & journeyed into the future –
which would be filled with a growing, steady melody;
layers of conformity…

but with some of that wonderful, disarranging
bullshit of youth

never completely fading away.

MARC BOLAN SANG

about life being an elevator ride –
up & down…

as children, we were taught in church
that *death is an elevator,* too:
up to Heaven
down to Hell.

that's an interesting piece
of emotional training.

whatever you believe,
that stays with you …

you walk through life,
crossing your fingers.

DO THE MATH

I'm often struck
by the power & beauty of Mathematics.
The   artistry
       symmetry
       balance

every child has to learn how many fingers they have ...
ancient Babylonians investigated how many degrees
there are in a circle...

go on:

jump straight into the whiteness of a blank page.
you may feel a temporary terror as you ponder,
work through, & solve a problem.
but, as you know – mathematical strategies & skills
are very handy in every day life.

e.g.

• we are all living Prime Numbers – divisible by
ourselves, & 1.
• she gave me about a Fraction of the affection I wanted.
• he was an Algebraic Problem I never understood.
• in societal terms, what is your Place Value?
• what is the Probability of living to 100?

• if the Universe is Infinite, how can it have a Square Root?

DRIVING WITH TERRY

the cassette tapes I play as I drive around the city
in my 1984 Toyota Corolla LE
are a dead man's tapes.

this music came into my hands because for several years
I was his daughter's number one squeeze.
he must have really liked this music, because these are all
homemade tapes, dubbed off original vinyl LPs.

the cardboard inserts inside each plastic cassette case
have playlists – in neat, upper-case handwriting.
I sing along with the music, & say things like:
'Good choice, Terry' – or
'Why did you pick that album, man? You know they
wrote better songs than that!'

if I'm on a downer – say I've fallen for somebody who
could out-flirt Madonna
& who now won't give me the time of day –
I'll pop one of his cassettes into the tape machine
& travel with him through the green lights to happier
distracted times.

lust is a bitch though
& the power of music brings those feelings –
the intense disappointment of unrequited dirty
thoughts to the surface.
Terry had been on that trip a few times
& sometimes, he's right there.

I often wonder which song was his favourite
on a particular album
& which particular part of that song really rocked his world.

e.g. on the tape containing *The Eagles – Greatest Hits,*
I wonder if he would have gone for "Take it to the Limit", "Lyin' Eyes",
or the masterpiece loved by millions: "Hotel California."

if it was the latter, I wonder whether his favourite part of the song would have been Joe Walsh and Don Felder's classic – Punk's-worst-nightmare-but-they'd-have-played-it-if-they-could solo interplay,
which cuts in just after Don Henley sings the line about checking out – but not being able to leave.

such is the esteem that this guitar solo is held in,
that it was voted the eighth-greatest guitar solo of all time by *Guitar* magazine.

Terry would have instinctively known he was listening to aural gold – a masterpiece of rock culture
because his taste in music was pretty good, overall.

an inspired guitar solo is like a joyful hit of liberation –
the creative inverse of emotional pain.

those who take their own lives can't get free of the pain
& express it in a drastically different way.
they get my respect.

those that don't understand
are lucky.

I've heard it:
'What a weak person'
'Good riddance'
'What a selfish thing to do' –

no understanding of how the human mind
can arrive in such a place –
the lake of fire; taking the freaking hand of
the Stygian Ferryman…

beyond anger.

they are the ones fortunate enough
to walk in the light
through pretty much all their lives.

those who don't –
get tired, desperate
& hear the call.

the music over.

EASTER POEM

watching a happy young boy
at Westfield Mall –

hungrily biting into & cracking
the shell of a white chocolate egg,

triggers recalled accounts
of young children's skulls

being split apart
by bombs

in Middle East marketplaces.
that's how things are these days.

PUSH IT

I invented a game called
"Think Up a Punk Band Name".

I came up with *The Rotting Nuns* –
disgusting everyone
(which was the point)
& which also
ended the game.

WAITING TO SEE IGGY & THE STOOGES

three young women

wrapped to ventilate
in summer dresses & sandals
were dancing in a field

shuffling rhythmic bodies
in licking, light blue
rain.

they appeared so utterly unfettered;
wonderfully alive
on the green grass.

& though so many things
lay waiting on the path ahead –
so many
many things

it seemed nothing was hiding from them
that afternoon.

the other thousands were already dissolving
into ordinary, unsaved history

while they were so sublimely
in the moment –

receiving signals from all the good places
& not afraid to show how that
felt.

I hope they remember.

THE DROWNPROOF MEN

that
Arabesque shape of light
between those trees
contains everything that is coming
& everything that has been

including the falling bodies
which are still falling
& will always be falling

& you –
carte blanche terror-franchise
delivery man
who grinningly caught the jock
pants down –

with your appropriated beard of
Islamic fire & brimstone
burning with reasons
& devoted volunteers.

our wake-up coffee?
two lumps of payback?
you're like a weird, old time schoolmaster
airing his fetid, curriculum daydreams
in public,

splashing around happily in the Ground Zero
tar pit –
the perfect cave man for the
new millennium.

& we made you ourselves –
our geo-political bogeyman
who 'loves death!'

can we touch you?
will you bite or spit?
shall we meet at an embassy, marketplace
or night club?

we listened to your spooky static
saw your fuzzy face on the terror news feed –
the media's special boy.

but what have you really taught our children?
that sarin gas smells like juicy fruit gum?

they'd rather smash piñata effigies of you
& kill you again & again
in games & games,

bid for your hair & skin
on eBay.

is it a good feeling – the ignition
of fresh blood in the earth?

it was an eerie tune – a single cutting note of
piano wire around the fat necks
of the dumb.

there were wonderful, demolition artefacts
scary extrapolations
teeming paranoia –
just a world-famous example of what governments
have always hidden?

well done,
gun-to-the-head man!
MTV's video of the decade award is yours.
but, were virgins really waiting
in the afterlife?

you certainly put a chill up the spine
of Bud & Coke drinkers everywhere –
getting spoiled, greedy little families
to move continents & sleep in global fear.

everyone hates a smug politician –
but you broke the golden rule:
don't kill the nice folk.

you parted those decadent, oily waters
like a prophet for the times
& watched the enemy rush straight in –

but you couldn't really control those waters.
they rushed back
icy & cold, over all our heads

& the drownproof men are coming.

GOING SOUTH

how many poems
can be written with your penis?

the women of Paris just laughed – busy enough
cleaning greasy ovens; the smell of fresh honey
seeping out from their pantries…

enough time spent
awkwardly walking cold, stone streets;
avoiding darkening puddles…

all I could do
was take a train ride south
alone –
yet another fake, young Baudelaire
without a mistress, nor even
a sick flower to clutch…

at least, I met an American girl in Marseilles –
with a wide, boozy smile, that said:
'People say you can't control your emotions –
the hell you can't!'

I didn't argue.

I only wanted her
to lie down across the continent –
so I could wash my dirty fingers
in the rivers
that flowed from her blue
Levis.

HOW I LEARNED TO LOVE MARGARITAS

the afternoon crack'd
like a thawing ice wall, releasing vapours of
wrung-out memory.

the snakes lay dead at the bottom.
it was time to move on.

the angle of a hill?
how you see it: a steep, mutant form – or
a slick escape route.

her fading, military-industrial-complex libido
had been part of the deal – her bare shoulders
once, scoops of warm dough.

our dialogue?
an oral document of fading commitment
based on initially good carnality.

& the love – it slowly transformed into damage
accompanied by the fast draining
of Margaritas.

the whole thing could easily be drawn on a tonal scale of
compatibility.

by the end
I may have replicated the most boring man on the planet
but in my mind

I could not be the Silver Surfer & Buddha
every day.

I WENT TO A PARTY WITH A PLATE OF OLIVES ON SATURDAY NIGHT & NOBODY WAS THERE

those yellow street lights like alien eyes
will be gone one day
& I will have been hurled thru
the answer as well.

it's such a pig of a thing –
greasy with handling; patterned with stab-holes
bleeding science
& theology –

right through the great, white veil of
nothing.

it's a pretty good question.

here, there's nobody at all
& not a sound inside this car –

which has the dark stillness of galaxies
for sale.

yet, my thought-meter is indicating
acceptance.

silence changes as you grow older –
spinning thru the atmosphere

curiously awaiting the shuddering end to life
& desired answer:

the seeing of what everything
really did mean.

tonight
I'll take the rain water
flicking off car tires, on the way home

instead of a room of nodding heads & full
stomachs – if that's all there is.
I'll take this quiet
& not seek anything –

maybe even ahead of God's hand waving
from the river.

BACK IN THE DAY

for Les Harvey

I knew a landlord millionaire who dressed like a scruffy old tugboat captain on shore leave, who liked to wander up & down the street, approaching middle-class women out shopping & recite The Bard to them. good old Will, no less. although his own stories would have been enough to hold them spellbound, he enjoyed the theatrical nature of the language & profound insight into the human condition.

he would gesticulate & perform for these women who were instantly trapped upon the paving stones outside the fancy boutiques that *he* in fact owned. they'd squirm with embarrassment – unable to do anything but endure the soliloquy & humour the "bum" before them, forced to listen. eventually, he would "release" them from his grasp & they would scurry away, with one or two backward glances – to continue their shopping, never realising the truth.

sly, rich old bugger.

DECISIONS AT THE MATA AIR FESTIVAL, SALITIGA

for Gita & Erwin

what is the name of that sleeping volcano –
making us want to suck deep on weed & ciu?

& what of these trees standing over us like guardians
of conversation & laughter?

enough questions already – this is a landscape of power,
but we also feel *tenang.*

each fact of existence dissolves
into a stream of affirmation –

sitting on soil, grass & leaves, we watch moments piggy-back
moments & exhale our responses:

Ucok the trumpet player, ums & ahs all day – to jam or
not – with spoken-word before finally admitting 'I just
wanted to get wasted'...

Deugalih plays his guitar, on which is a version of
Guthrie's mantra:
this machine turns losers into healers & sings about the drugs
not working anymore...

DJ Sampson – spinning vintage vinyl 45s, chooses an
obscure erotic track from '69
& the orgasmic moans of a woman fill our forest...

Tony – jungle photographer, is busy with bubble
mixture, seeking to capture
the ultimate sunburst...

Nova simply obliterates a heckler who shouts at her to get off the stage – her voice soaring, carrying…

PainSugar says he kissed goodbye to God seventeen years ago
& he's doing fine…

INSTRUCTION PIECE

after Yoko

buy one clock for every year you have lived.

insert 1 dead AA battery in each one.
set the hands at midnight.
hang them all on one wall in a grid-like fashion.
now buy a clock for the current year & working batteries
so it will run for 365 x 24.
i.e. TICK TOCK TICK TOCK TICK TOCK

repeat this for each coming New Year.

e.g. You might have 35 "dead" clocks on a wall, with a
single one running, ticking, counting down …

IRISH BAR IN TAKAPUNA

poems
are stolen from the ether
        & transferred to the page:

the
steaming
world –

a collection
of canopic jars –
                    theatrical
                            & dirty,
shrugged at
by wide-eyed immortal children –
already aware of politics
& boredom in the churches.

here
the bow sweeps across the fiddle
& an accordion squeezes
out the tears –

Johnny's the fairest man

everything will change
where does the piece go?

dismantle humanity's
intricate maze
                of pathways,
over
a pint of beer.

POSTCARD – WAITANGI DAY AT THE NZ EMBASSY

Gidday! Well, there we were – 7000k from home on Waitangi Day, rising into the "balmy" airspace above Jakarta (13 million people!!) to the air-conditioned Kiwi Embassy up a high-rise, looking down on the little people. Ha-ha! Not that we got big heads. Out of the lift, past dear Mr Key hanging on the wall, into the mix 'n' mingle room, where there were one or two suits at ease & a spread – saveloys, white bread cheese sandwiches, spring rolls – like my old church back in the 70's! Were they taking the piss? We wondered. Drinks? Deal was you forked over 90,000 Rupiah (got that??) for a voucher – gave you 2 glasses of wine *or* 6 beers – all Kiwi brands. Bit disappointing it wasn't on the house, to be honest, mate. The beer calculation – which we all did, worked out at about $1.80 NZ per, so I guess it was a pretty good deal. Get into it? We did, mate – working the room! Doing the dance – the Asian Hustle! Ha-ha! & glad to be on carpet– it's a marble floor paradise here. Oh – & broken fuckin' footpaths everywhere, mate – in need of a few council workers. Met this Kiwi cement guy actually, who produces a LOT of cement in Jakarta. (Not bloody footpaths, I thought to myself – ha-ha) What did he say? 9 x the volume of cement produced in Kiwiland! A shitload of cement, mate! & he's only a *minor* player. Who else? Some dude called "Baldy" who's lived here for 37 years – married a local, still calls himself a Kiwi – fair enough. Talked trade with an embassy bloke – word is 'Europe's over', mate. It's all Asia now! Any babes? – I hear you ask ☺ 2 young "Indo" darlings employed by the embassy – no beer goggles required, mate! & the only non-Kiwis there. Finally, out came this bloody huge, bloody thick cheesecake (no Pavlova) swamped with strawberries, just as the beer ran out. Did I help myself? Mate! Yeah, that was Treaty day. To be honest, the only time the word "Maori" popped into my head was when I met this Tainui guy who builds golf courses over here. I even got to borrow the ambassador's id tag for the staff toilet. Nice bloke, nice toilet. Checked for cameras! Ha-ha! Yeah, that was us, mate – a bunch of happy, high-flying Kiwis who busted out, having a right-good piss-up on Waitangi Day, but we never did talk about home!

WHAT *IXTAB* – THE MAYAN GODDESS OF SUICIDE – WHISPERED TO ME

had enough of life's windmill of flying fists? too many rides on the human 'coaster? sick of love, happy pills & councillors? life does *not* have to end in old age in a hospital bed, waiting…

Handgun:

fast. if careful, face left intact. nicer for friends and relatives. they can just bear to look at you in the coroner's room…

Jump off a building:

freefall to splattersville. the higher the building, the longer you fall & bigger the bang as your body-bag explodes. no turning back, once you jump. go out like a fucked-up stuntman screaming through the wind, or try for a completely silent one-with-the-universe thing. but messy: we're talking shovels & hoses…

Thelma & Louise:

one last extreme, lawless, theme park ride! you decide whether you grip the steering wheel staring through the windscreen, or lie back on recline, eyes shut, wondering how many seconds left. maybe a big BOOM & flames if you're lucky. professional supervision not recommended. just properly check out the damn cliff-face. half-dead ain't it…

Airstrike:

not really available, unless you have serious contacts – but how cool would it be? take a last walk & then call in the co-ordinates. you'd get to hear the delivery man above your head & maybe see the snuff-device coming straight at you. desert or beach might be best. yell a bit of bullshit & then wait for nirvana. they could probably patch you through to the rellies, if you wanted...

IT WAS THE DAY

it was the day the bombs fell on Iraq –
no, it wasn't.

it was the day I first heard life described as a "jailbreak" –
no, it wasn't .

it was the day I drank beer at school instead of going to
prize-giving assembly –
no, it wasn't.

it was the day my boss quietly snarled 'Do you
understand the expression – *don't bite the hand that feeds*?' –
no, it wasn't.

it was the day somebody stole my blue dungarees & a
$30 hooker left her earrings in my flatmate's bed –
no, it wasn't.

it was the day the TV said John Lennon was dead –
no, it wasn't.

it was the day my neighbour Lorraine gave her nipples
away to a sailor named Dave –
no, it wasn't.

it was the day my wife threw away my Edmund Hilary
& Sherpa Tensing autographs –
no, it wasn't.

it was the day my friend Mark kicked in the radiator of
a mutual friend's car & said 'He was always going to get

his radiator kicked in' –
no, it wasn't.

it was the day a burning cigarette was pushed into the
back of my leg –
no, it wasn't.

it was the day some phlegm on the footpath was shining
like an illumination from God –
no, it wasn't.

IT WOULD BE A STRANGE FUNERAL

I heard the gears of the universe one night –
howling & screaming in pain

while waiting for a train in a Spanish Railway station.

the ancient tracks outside sounded like they were
breaking apart
as box cars floated past the windows, full of filthy hoboes
crying luminescent tears.

the heavy station doors were bashed open & then
slammed shut by the jackboot wind
& then bashed open & then slammed shut again.

a giggling whore sat nearby, licking a long silver bullet
& a drunk rhinoceros walked into the room, offering me a
drink.

it was a normal night at Figueres railway station.
exactly what I should have expected – waiting for a train

only a short distance from where Dali lay ill in his bed,

awaiting the surrealism
of death.

THE MOVIE BUSINESS

if I'm having one of those seriously wrong
time-place-me days,
I still couldn't say goodbye
to the sun.

because I'm supposed to be here – right?
& the open-ended nature of life (the hook)
works pretty well.

of course, we're *all* in the movie business:
with the actors, the setting, the lighting, the script…
either trying to avoid – or maintain
the ordinary & predictable.

sometimes things feel odd, out of place.
sometimes you want to push, test –
rearrange what there is; give it a little bit of drama
– like the Motorcycle Boy
in *Rumble Fish* –

breaking into that pet shop & trying to put those fish
back in the river.

LOST & FREE ON A STREET IN JAKARTA

in the moment!

one more evacuee
from a hundred million moments

zigzagging in rain – among strange rubbish, dirt,
busted concrete, & revving monster motorcycle-mash of
commuters...

I was seeking a pathway home, in a smoky blue dusk
& failing as only a foreigner can – absolutely!
to hail a taxi...

yet, there was laughter inside my aching heels;
sanctuary inside the eyes of the riders,

as I started to unfold that old Siddhartha Gautama stuff
about our thoughts making the world –

& curiosity felt good
walking further up the number line than I had for quite a
while...

easy words, familiar ghosts
left behind

replaced by

new doorways
tickets to shadow plays
calls to prayer.

LOVE BUTTONS

Sam Hunt had control of the rainbows.

for a while
I had control of your light show:
pressing the buttons gently, to watch the colours
run.

it was a lucky accident –
because we were verbally discordant.
& God forbid,
if I said the wrong thing.

all hell would break loose, as you began to shriek your
head off.

then it would be wrong button, after wrong button
as the dark, molten blanket came down

& hot, psychic hail
piled up inside my ringing ears.

I'd stand there – a mixture of embarrassment & shock
while trying to understand –
putting up with the din of all dins
in all of the Shaky Isles.

for love.
plain, simple love
& for what you later told me
was ordinary sex.

M&Ms

I was walking into the city, thinking of dunes of sand
like some kind of preferred, empty land.

sure, there's poverty about feeling disconnected –
not plugged into the communal switchboard,
but there's also relief.

today, we're all supposed to be on the same page;
so bloody well informed – in the social jewellery

of poise, knowledge
& demeanour –

our articles of agreement.
our meal of behaviour.

for a while it's quite easy to fit in,
then one day you might find yourself having to chew on
the world a hell of a lot longer than you used to –
& swallowing is a little harder…

you remember the early days,
carrying that wonderful bag of nothing over the
shoulder;
not belonging anywhere.

you think of these things when
you're

frequently stubbing your toe on roads that once led to
evenings of endorphin blue…

counting cars at night
as the lonely wind bashes into the roof…

eating M&Ms, one after another –
seeking a sugary, astral plane.

METHOD

swallow wine

of magic roots,

at the hanging

of boredom.

MONEY $HOT

the broken ones, the busted ones
the shivy, shabby, shum
are out there on the footpath
proving they are scum.

if birds of judgement sweep too low
it hardly does surprise –
empathy is fleeting
from those with buttered eyes.

the celebration of the buck
is alive everywhere –

in the penthouses & caves,
school & work,
fucking,
& in the bugle call of every country.

money –
is a soul-balm which kicks religion's ass
right out of the spiritual park!

money –
is the most successful form of communication
ever invented

& even those bums on the street – many of whom choose
to reject the system

are constantly calculating what they are
worth.

MOTORWAY POEM

I was travelling down the motorway reading a book
& as each sentence disappeared
over my shoulder

I fell into the thing where
time only exists because each moment
dies.

I was sitting in my car – but not really

& trying to hold onto
that moment – but knowing
that moment was already gone, too.

time –
an emissary from the future
saying you're already history

but also, our greatest hero
dying endlessly
                              & endlessly reborn –

the way children keep appearing:
hand-made sons & daughters
of emperor eternity

who are then plucked from
the cosy nest of time –

to get old & wise
on these endlessly vanishing
roads.

MY MY HEY HEY

for Eden

I didn't learn the concept about old things being good
from Neil Young,
but from
an episode of *The High Chapparal*.

what I did learn from Neil
is that
if someone throws a bunch of coins in your face
during a quiet acoustic number,
immediately stop playing!

throw down your guitar,
eyeball the front row –
scaring the shit out of them,
scream:
'Who did that?'
& storm off stage!

then, after a short break,
you come back, say nothing,
plug in for the electric set,
work up into a frenzy,
&
R O C K,

with massively loud, full-on,
angry & defiant,

b
e
a
u
t
i
f
u
l
l
y

s t r u c t u r e d

N
O
I
S
E

reminding everyone
just exactly
WHO IS BOSS!

but, you finish up with a few
good ol' Neil grins,
just so they still want to go out
& buy some more records
on Monday morning.

PHILOSOPHY

shall we seek Satan's help when the aliens come?

POLISHING THE CONCRETE

cold footpath passes beneath my feet –

the task of pushing gradient
will eventually be complete.

fleeing last night's conversation
each sad step is a mental harmonica
blues –

a striving for honesty…
like the first bus of the morning.

that tricky heart will soon be waking –
but Ghostface Killah says

fuck that shit.

maybe
I'll let somebody else blow air into that balloon

let it go
& empty my pockets

let it go
& watch her do that ascension thing –
high above the hard concrete.

WOMAN IN PRISON

her favourite thing
was listening to the *Death Wish II* soundtrack
composed by Jimmy Page
while painting beach scenes from her imagination.

she was something of a starved libertine – but drew
the line at some of the prison pastimes:

"I wasn't into debauching young girls –
I missed screwing, but I made do with the ol'
handiwork."

she'd found calm distraction from over-thinking
thru the "audio-chocolate high" of the radio-waves
shaped & formed
by the spectacularly decadent & fading rock star –
Mr Page

& pushing ocean blue & sand-coloured oils around
on canvas.

"I learned my lesson while doing time – shaping every
moment of regret into a little badge of transformation.
I've stopped being naughty; stopped reaching for what I
don't need..."

she tells me all this
while slowly smoking a joint on her bed
in Autumn darkness –

three days before she walks into the surf at
her favourite beach
& drowns.

SAFETY DEPOSIT BOX

we spent crazy
misshapen
                    ringing

yet, oddly muted hours
together.

thousands of them.

how strange to see them
suddenly stop
shrink
& fit so neatly
into this small time-capsule

floating before my eyes.

The Past:
contained, sealed –
always in front
& ready for contemplation

just as ancient Asian prophets
said it would be.

&
The Future:
uncertain, eerily prospective
rushing

sneaking up fast
behind me.

SEEKING THE ANSWERS IN WESTERN PARK

for Tim Heath

this could be a place to hide
from the tortures of love, guilt, or fear
(it's in the city, after all)
but, not today.

those things are only the warm-up:
the itch that proves we're alive.

I'm just taking a brief, mental vacation,
a psychic chill-pill – from Concreteland
to ponder the Big Question.
the one we're all pondering.

What's it all about, dude?

this is a good place to think.
a manicured, primeval forest
with a handy downhill / uphill gradient:
nice & symbolic

with
scattering young children,
millions of tiny, trained dogs,
a few snoozing, Scandinavian backpackers
& skiving business men & women.

no doubt – all secretly, deep in the subliminal
the subtext:
Heaven?

the odd, fully-equipped
protein-packed, intellectual city athlete
is working it hard through here –
no doubt getting that body trained
to filter as much life as possible.

this place is also a bum's room – on a golden scale,
with empty liquor bottles & the odd used condom
scattered among the leaves,
& sure –
there's knowledge to be gained in sex & booze!

in the distance, I spot an iPod-packing troll
among trees shaped like strange inquiries into
what on earth we're doing.

sometimes, I just can't get away from it.

I pass the obligatory couple, enjoying their soul-
searching love-cloud
on bough-shaded paths.

tree theology in abundance!
they drop delicate carcasses of experience.
their growing branches are the shape of things to come,
like sentences from the future.
do they have eyes?
do they have souls?

their biggest fear?
chainsaw attack, idiot!
they needn't fear me – I'm not even going to sit
under one of them, & write
Zen poetry!
although, if I don't
that is Zen, too.

it's inspiring enough to walk the Balance Incline beam,
like a nimble, photoelectric cell
sent from the giant light bulb in the sky.
born to vanish!

I feel like that French guy on the tightrope
dancing between the Twin Towers,
who was arrested
& subsequently screwed by a female admirer.

he must have had some kind of vision, up there!
the balancing act of life:
What's real & what's a dream?

it'd be good to zap those orbiting scythes
committing sonic murder above…
but now I'm busy – spying on 3 men at a round table.
are they praying, or confessing?
something has happened,
or, is about to.
perhaps they know.

I strain to listen,
but a nearby bell rings, & schoolgirls run screaming,
radiantly
back to class.

my visit to the park is over, too.
maybe
that's the answer.

KEMANG RAYA WALK

shiny face me – out & about
walking uphill Saturday am thru frequently-ill sunshine
& steaming blue smoke –
flower stalls, motorbike babies, rotting rubbish,
orange & black bajajs, oversize Stupid Ugly Vehicles
& 3rd dead rat of week – nicely squashed: guts squeezed out –
like the poor here in Indonesia…

spot trainer tread-pattern on fresh speed-bump paint –
bright yellow, stick-man in white paint on ground
& wall graffiti – head of man w/- wings – meaning?
eye-candy – always plenty…

as I turn right onto Kemang Raya – boulevard of
crumbled footpath, perfumed dust, street-food &
carbonated petrol clouds –
hard on the streets here
stride / cough, don't breathe, must breathe – avoid new
hole in ground, furry grey water – don't fall in –

whistles & shouting –
"Terus! Terus!" Keep going! Keep going!

& they will –
election over / banners down –
new boss – an end to corruption / big business /
military dominance?
– precautionary water cannon & tanks still on streets…

the people wait –
& I think about them,
as I step into franchised unreality: coffee at Starbucks –
skim milk Latte tall, chocolate muffin, upstairs soft chair,
AC, note paper…

THE ART OF FAILURE

for Shane Hollands

the doors on the bus work well in summer –
shutting 27 degrees outside
while the air-conditioning does its cool feminine
crawl over me –
a passenger:
riding Zen wheels; breaking
from the scorching *poetry psychosis (!)*
outside

where the sweat drips
& the task remains.

thru the window – liquid leaves
on unhugged politically safe trees of the city
v-i-b-r-a-t-e…
they want attention, too…
but they only need eyes.

landscapes are just so much easier to deal with.
who cares who the great landscapers of history are?
why stand still & stare at somebody's garden
watching it slowly die?

we have enough problems constructing the perfect dispatch –
one that does the *Nagasaki* all over
'The Good Life.'

sure
I've got my ass nailed down:
picked the spot, hammered in the nails
& know I'm only as free
as one of those leaves…

but I can *think* any way I want
& the doors on the bus will open again –
somewhere up the road.

I'll be back out there in the heat – the creative Hell
arc-welding letters together
& also confronting *Beauty* –
the other monster

which has never been truly defined –
driving people mad for years.

it empties me out – being so hooked…
in awe of something so elusive.

I think I'll just tip my hat again to Picasso –
he could swear in paint
without writing a single word.

THE DARK CRACKS OF KEMANG

oxygen boils in the lungs of geckoes
as unborn prototypes squirm in warm soil.

the search for sex is a reciprocate game
on thin streets,

where broken footpaths have fallen
from the minaret tower

& love might be a piece of rusted steel filigree.

here, black coffee sweats slowly out thru skin –
as light brown legs walk thru crosshairs

& floodwater is quivering
in deep, dark cracks.

the key?

you get the feeling – that it's money
or, you dig what you want, straight out of
the ground.

the bajaj drivers eat noodles & wait
in mauve rain,

clothes get hand-sewn in back alleys,

& the gecko eyelids enclose each
moment.

THE KING

Rimbaud
did not really know about
senescence,
anno domino,
old age.
his work has the perspective
of a young person
typically challenging,
defiantly laughing at death.

he basically knew fuck-all
about getting old,
even dying at 37 himself.

in fact, he reigned himself in,
believing at 20 that he had nothing
left to say.

what a relief to just live.
let the senses feel, with no creative mining
of experiences.

no justification or questioning, or panic
over completion of some never-ending
romantic notion, from the dark corners of your mind.
but, how can you stop writing at 20?
there was no excuse.

he took the easy way out.

THE METAL INSIDE OUR HEADS

that buzzing sound?
residuals, maybe – from the electrical explosions
inside.

I reached up into the sky & snatched furiously at
the dust of old dreams
to see if that might dampen the noise.

it was either that
or turn the volume knob up to 10
& dance – not admitting defeat
but accepting that you cannot
want things without paying:

tangible possibilities –
floating in the live current.

THE MISSING CHILD

your pixel face –
on the surface of a pool

crisscrossed by dragonflies,
beneath a talking sky, full of Allah –

a contemplation.

life put me here – a journey apart
in a movement thru air & water:

a rhythm of memory & longing –
faster than breathing, slower
than drowning…

a father's lesson.

I think it worked like this:

I gave you my version of the world –
which you slowly no longer needed…

which is how it should be.

you grew into yourself
& are now setting off – through the tunnels of the world

with your flashlight & guitar,
to make your own meanings

& send your music up thru
the air.

TOMORROW?

I do nothing that might
influence, shape, or affect
it in any way.

I live each day as a complete,
self-contained unit of time!

if I die tonight,
I've done everything I could.

Picasso: a girl, wine & food, friends, one painting.
one revolution of the earth.

FOGGING

they're fogging the grounds – right on schedule,
as birds cross the perimeter of the window.

on my bed, your cones of warm flesh
point downriver, beneath boughs stuffed with
question marks…

it's probably a good spot –
to put down the blanket, again hear that naughty
chuckle as you count off the orgasms;
share homemade tuna salad & beer;
test what we have…

you'd say those things like
"Do you see my face in your mind?"

& I'd think to myself:
"Is it her?"

WAITING FOR DIAMONDS TO CRY

my grandfather's words –
"There, but for the grace of God, go I"

are all over this human mess
surely squeezed up thru some fissure in the
underworld –
a body squealing

each eye like a Bruegel boil –
one angled at God,
the other scanning the boulevard for benefactors
or mere trouble.

his twisted mouth sucks air – in time
with a jangling tin cup & chain –

it's impossible to look away.
I don't think of violins, but rip saws going

thru bone.
three laughing, walking machine guns

say they want to hire the finest whore in Paris –
just to watch her suck your cock.

oh, the world's as hard as rock.
one key should fit every lock

but nobody cares
& some have a long wait for death.

BALI satu

fooled by a leaf – not a moving rat
but a dead organism

on its way home.
nervous in the colour-wheel Sanur night –

the air thick with trees
& fake glowing tiger eyes.

the Armagideon TIMES sits in bright yellow light
on distressed wood –

stained with
mosquito poison & beer

& I think of Mr Blake
who put me here.

BALI dua

the poetry machine crawls across the sky

puff, click, whir, fade…

does the mind ever sleep?
Apakah pikiran pernah tidur?

the mind never sleeps
Pikiran tak pernah tidur

the mind
Pikiran itu

the mine
tambang

BALI tiga

slab of glass with trickle of lime juice.
cane wicker chair & what's left of an afternoon.

saya mau means I want –
coffee & Monte Crysto sandwich,

as young wanita in purple sarong decorates a prayer
with flowers.

the fat Germans are swimming again –
blue eyes searching the pool for *Gelassenheit.*

it's feeding time too, for the school of fish
at the Sukun Bali Cottage

& they move in a brutal water-tattoo.
somewhere is a design:

trillions of intersecting lines.
the spirograph spins –

a motorcycle rider delivers a parcel;
nearby, someone starts drilling a hole.

my task is to finish eating
& return cup to saucer.

& that's it for now – except for staff whispering
in Bahasa; Hindu temples in my coffee grounds.

BALI empat

swim in heat of Bali
dance in crooked taksi

look high & low
for the author of 'Rimbaud in Java'

the journey might be shit –
but the end could be *nirvana*

BALI lima

ah, the strangling of birds in the morning –
just a mood?

Ganesha is smiling –
covered in lichen & mould, bathed
in incense.

I suppose you would
if you were dead – murdered

& then had an elephant's head
stitched onto your own

decapitated body
& brought back to life?

WHIMSICAL VEGETABLES

the city –
just so much traffic & seagulls; mechanical gestures
coated in psychic energy.

the moving parts of life swirl in yellow oil
thru car windscreens
& shopping lists ricochet inside skulls of
thought.

there's hope in that feeling of sun on the steering wheel –
turning warmly thru the choices…

& there's satisfaction in calm routine –
waiting for a new strategy

to lift yourself thru the synchromesh & truly connect
to the big family – whatever that is.

there's pleasure – burning fat in calm self-forgiveness,
revisiting ribbon-breaking moments
that seemed to drip from an alternate, better reality
which never openly declared itself.

in altruistic moments, you can always
chew on the hope inside jam sandwiches
while you daydream at traffic lights:

is the world suddenly in love
with caring & kindness?

or
is that just an impression –
some new trend soaked up from the streets?

a classic social recipe:
mix in a few grimaces, over coffee & balsamic vinegar

all of it becoming just so many whimsical vegetables
chopped up for dinner; printed on newspaper;
sold on a hook in the markets?

the light changes.

HE'S GOTTA SEE US, HE'S GOTTA STOP

the last words spoken by James Dean
in his Porsche Spyder, which was going fast –
heading straight towards the intersection
but really – heading way beyond that.

Jimmy knew he wasn't going to stop.
he never had.

the poetry of collision –
something dies & something new is born.

Jimmy was a barely known Hollywood actor
who frequently pissed off his male lovers
& brought crabs to the set of *Rebel Without A Cause*.
he was moody, insular & wild.

how many days of living do you
fit into 24 hours?
you know those moments when you pull back.

there's a fear of moving, unconnected energies…
a fear of impact.

most of us turn away from uncertainty.
we buy safety to rest our heads, but the true spirit inside
wants to run

& taste
& leap
& land beyond the familiar.

we can't help it.
most of us slow down & prepare to stop, when we
approach an intersection.
leaving nothing to chance –

already dead.

1977

one evening –
lying under a fresh cool bed sheet,

I dropped the stylus
onto
the
vinyl

& listened to the famous side 2
of *Abbey Road* –

drifting off to sleep
in sublime, flawless relaxation.

I awoke – with a wonderful
sensation –
HIGH and ALIVE!

every part of my body felt
I N C R E D I B L E

I floated through my morning routine
in glorious spring light.

it seemed hardly possible:
it wasn't a case of 'everything in harmony & balance'
or any of that shit

I walked through the city streets
in
S H O C K E D   A M A Z E M E N T:

I was ready
for the world.

it was truly
A S T O U N D I N G
&
it never happened again.

DYING PLANET SUPERHEROES

is Earth as wounded as we think?
have we fucked things up as royally as
we believe?

worse, you say?
but now we know where we're going?
we know what to do?

do we look back and thank
those who lived 50 years ago?
100? 500?

saving the world for tomorrow
is against the historical flow of
humanity.

aren't we marvellous?

WORKING IN OBSCURITY / DYING OUTSIDE ETERNITY

for Jack Micheline

Ozzy vocals weave around palm trees at Venice
& I'm on *BROOKS,* with the triple S:

sun! surf! sand! & "breakfast muffin w/- Canadian
bacon" at *Sidewalk* – making notes.

Andy would add: "$33.00 cab fare from *LAX*" –
which is fair enough, but the morning coffee issue is:

what do you get for a life of work?

an 8am blonde with a broom sweeps concrete nearby
& considers her fate,

as bits of Biggie Smalls float in the haze.
party-train vendors haul hand-made art for sale

as expensive leisure clothing swans past
wanting you to think FAT never looked sexier, aging
avoidable –

& it's fashionably true, biologically not.
the pavement piano man warms up with a few
extravagant gestures –

soon cut to pieces in the blades of the po' chopper
& the waft of a doobie nicely completes the setting.

suddenly, the ultimate showman arrives:
spitting & yelling angry non-sequiturs –

his words are golden hammers tossed into air.
you can watch him squeeze thru the sieve –

without a care.

THINK IT, BUT DON'T SAY IT

the Swastika …

is usually banned.
but you can still use the symbol,
if you can culturally or artistically
justify its use.

& it has a guaranteed audience –
whatever you think.

phonetically speaking –
it's still a cool word to say.

visually –
still a cool symbol to draw.

whisper it softly to yourself,

or draw it carefully with a pencil
on crisp, white paper.

can you deny the guilty pleasure?

BAD DINNER PARTIES

it's partly knowing you just don't belong there; fit in.
partly something about
measuring up, social judgement.

& something to do with how you view
yourself.

balance is a concept we are supposed to aim for, or
already possess,
but it can take years to achieve.

it's mostly about dealing with people – but being with them
can constantly upset the process of learning.

a room full of talking faces may produce intense
feelings of isolation & anxiety.

& when the teaspoon clattered on the marble floor
& you knew you didn't want to bring your head back up
to the table
& hold the eyes
& you were still affected by old comments:

you always get frightened when you are put in a corner
you have the brain of a pussy cat
you need to take stock of your life –

oh, that wonderful moment:

the glorious walking out of the room –
like Janet Frame.

SELF-INTERVIEW

answer the following question:

WHO r u ?

include details of what you have
DONE, what you are WANTING to
do, etc.

if it is too overwhelming, find the nearest swamp
& start draining it.
this physical metaphor should help
to clarify your mind,
& help you decide if it is really worth getting up
off your ass.

or, whether you like being stuck in the swamp.

TRAITOR

just because
I am a New Zealander
doesn't mean
that I can't
prefer the landscape, smog,
& architecture
of L.A.
& the fact that
David Lynch's *Cinema of Unease*
is better than ours.

THE BUMS HAVE STYLE

for Jay

in the theatre of the streets,
who is he?
grubby character actor?
broken
leading
man?
walking
flexible
trash
can?

I saw him! – arm dipped
in
fresh
garbage
(his own private mini-mart)

ankle-deep in the crushed chewing gum & ciggie-butts –
with a glorious stench
wafting into the perfumes & after-shaves of the city
élite.

his voice?

I heard a politician say I should be
hosed off the streets. That's gonna work!

Let's all pretend that society is that simple!
Hey, if I have the floor,
Everything I do is a metaphor

for all the other metaphors I see walking around –
living their little obsessive lives – accumulating, pontificating!

Oh yeah, I used to work in an office!
Dumb, middle class sheep!
B a a a a ! . . .

RAINY SEASON POEM

it was a week of stolen umbrellas
free Valentine's Day chocolate & secondary smoke
a lonely barking dog
& time spent getting over another mountainous cold.

I was too busy slicing carrot & cucumber
to notice how each day quietly thickened,
wrapping itself around neighbourhood concrete towers –
just before it absolutely pissed down.

I'd forgotten the way rain is held in the sky 'til the very
last moment – like a longed-for, overdue message.
a change felt imminent,
but I couldn't see beyond this whirling collective...

coffee-drinking at Starbucks, set to *Adagio in G Minor*
jumping frogs on jagged paths
smiling gardeners in the wet foliage
rats the size of cats, eating garbage
a shitload of monkeys swinging thru the trees
men hand-pulling nails out of wood
& friends moving to Bali –

a forensic scoop of life!
as it turned out, there was no need
to predict / fixate on the future –
the rain was enough.

it was an old year still falling,
& I kissed the residue
& waited.

WHITE NAPKINS

I was waiting for a text
one floor above the street, in an expensive restaurant
while a house version of the musical theme from *Last
Tango in Paris* played.

this is what life is now – waiting for texts & drinking
expensive coffee, watching the frozen watercolour morning
thaw.

the music made me remember what Marlon Brando was
doing to Maria Schneider in the movie & what she
was doing to him.

he made her go get the butter; she made him finally
fall for her – too late.

the music also got me in the mood to think about
the issue of how long you should wait,
with head & heart engaged.

drinking expensive coffee
& just visualising tits, pussy, hair all over my face
was the easy alternative.

the white napkins on the table seemed perfectly at ease –
folded, pressed, unused.

WAITING FOR THE NEWS

every sunset
our magnetic ball of luminosity
rolls away –
as if dragging memos to burn on the other side.

our brains – purged?
not quite.
each cell remains as full as a dirt hill –
full of history & affectation.

you might have an empty house though
with a soft, leather chair
for sitting & humming "Bohemian Rhapsody"
or some other burlesque interpretation
of what it all means.

the breathing of air?

your reason to diarize – more
activity which appears to have no meaning –
once famously described
& probably the best way to test any
explanation.

something powerful did a similar thing once –
fiddling around building us
& most of the universe,

& once the system's rolling
you can piss off & do something else –
which is pretty much what happened,

leaving people to come up with their version
of the big bang; file memories.

wouldn't *you* sell everything down the fucking river
to know the truth?

I WAS VIBRATING IN THE NEON SANDWICH OF THE AMERICAN LANDSCAPE

I was vibrating in the neon sandwich of the American landscape –
breathing/beating/b-ing – ready to take what was coming & plenty was – including a vegan chocolate pudding & a *Time* magazine cover about the protest movement. I didn't want to get angry every time I saw an expensive car or avocado pear but I nodded slyly with my upgraded knowledge – mostly to the billboards & bums & carried on my way, wondering out loud: WHAT THE HELL DOES FREEDOM MEAN, ANYWAY? WHAT *IS* A GOOD LIFE, THESE DAYS? & DIDN'T IT *ALL* GO TO SHIT AFTER THE KILLING OF JFK?

it was me socio-political thinking with sideways head – on red, white & blue checkerboard bed – back in America, the country I wanted to live in - from the moment I started watching television.

what was the current vibe in America? There were clues at LAX – where I admired a girl's nerve for putting on a hula-hoop show, scanned Hollywood souvenirs, & smiled at seeing *KISS* on the cover of *Rolling Stone*. old-fashioned showbiz alive & well. in the coffee shop, a nuclear power plant instructor urged me to visit Big Sur, Yellowstone, The Grand Canyon & Death Valley. in America you automatically believe that everything *will* happen – like that cool fool swimming pool Gatsby.

LAX to Texas was on an American Airlines no-terror-plane & before I knew it I was shovelling midnight cherry pie into my mouth, using Tea Tree Therapy brand mint-flavoured toothpicks & studying a 19th century Edward S Curtis calendar photo of an Indian "mother & child". on the wall were twisted neon sticks of lime green, ruby-red & purple, a screen-print of a black silhouette of a hand, which the artist had surrounded by staring elongated eyes, & I fell asleep with mental re-runs of *Zero Dark Thirty* – lights out for Mr X. the future was always written.

it was good to be back – soaking in the source: the American-ness of everything, home of deep 60s /70s psychic-infiltration of myself. as a kid I was always impressed: when you met an American, you really met them.

first day – my friends & I hiking down a limestone trail, remembering the Alamo – just like Sam Houston wanted & surprising a snake on the path – which quickly slithered up a tree & seemed to watch us in a biblical way. & indeed, it did appear to be a neighbourhood of miracles, affirmations: I witnessed the ballet of a cockroach miming to wind-chime melodies, watched a man imbibing animal fat – whose body could only be described as a circle with sticks, saw a blond-haired mom-angel give loving neighbourly support to a dying war veteran, & conversed with car-accident paraplegic Fred, who easily out-smiled me & declared 'Every day is a great day'. a default plan: to be happy / six senses set free in a vast economy.

one morning: walking up the street in 75° beneath Blue Jay on telephone wires – a black & white swerves & angles me to the spot – 'You seen this kid? He's not dangerous or anything – he just took off!' / 'No, never seen him'. amble a bit further in clear sunlight, watching an overall man play lonely leaf-blower blues.

one evening: watching Longlegged Sac spider climb another Hank Williams purple sky & hearing voices: 'Pain without consequence is not such a big deal', 'Just can't make no money', 'It's easy to hide in book stores – harder to give it all up & help the poor' & 'America's not a community. America is a business!'

& what of affluent middle-aged men meeting at hip joint for coffee? – sweet bullshit & jibes, sports-talk, Obama – proposed discretionary spending budget:
food & agriculture 1%, transportation 2%, science 3%, international affairs 3%, energy & environment 3%, social security, unemployment, labour 5%, Medicare & health 5%, housing & community 5%, government 6%, veterans benefits 6%, education 6%, military 55%.

on Sixth Street, red-eyed fly bums block sidewalk as part-time musicians play "How long has this been going on?" / in the glow of a Shiner Bock beer, I drink to friends who hate America for geo-political reasons & wish they could sit with me & listen to Chuck Berry & Bo Diddley on the jukebox.

& late afternoon notes: listened to freight-train horns & thought of hobos & Neal Cassady / bought last jar of Folgers instant at local gas station & last carton of half-&-half – craving cup of Joe / favourite meal: chicken salad w/- olives – in empty outdoor room of white table cloths covered with leaves.

everything was a defining moment – you just had to pick which one you wanted:

two musician friends:
"How are things?"
"Ah…"
"Play me something."

AS HAPPY AS ARION SINGING TO PERIANDER, AS SAD AS ORPHEUS LOSING EURYDICE

'Don't worry about it!' – friend Nick, thirty-odd years ago.
he was right.
but there was no way to stop the notion that things just didn't always feel OK.
it seemed I hadn't been properly trained in life!
but everything was already rolling, according to the ancient formula:

ignorance + desire + fear + accidental happenings + pain + TV + alcohol – set in a small milieu of strangers, colleagues & friends.

I didn't recite *OM AH HUM*. I couldn't say *OM AH HUM*. I hadn't even heard of *OM AH HUM*.

I wasn't really blaming anyone or where I'd come from – it was just that it appeared completely peculiar how life worked.
what were we?

post-modern fools on God's grainy Super 8?
beggars & shotgun-raiders of humanity's inventory?
drinkers of fast-moving pedagogy? –
either the hold yer nose & swallow type or the freestyler who appeared to swim happily in the stuff…

it all seemed to be a monstrous sea of flickering words & pictures.
I would never really fit in.
Or it would take a very long time.

who was I?

just another naive, young kid
grasping at life,
at poetry.

DIE BELIEVING

I was at the crucifixion of Jesus.

if you were a kid at my Sunday school –
you were taken to see the whole thing.

there was no thought about trying to stop it.
you just watched the Romans go into action;
considered their propaganda:

here is a guy who is promising too much,
getting a little too famous.

people were arguing about the reasons
& it was hard to tell how many people truly cared.
mass protest? hardly.

there were many trying to stand up & be the way –
speechmakers, weird witchdoctor types…

we heard the stories about what he'd done – the fish;
the money; how the mud people were going to get everything.
I never saw anything first-hand.

people were often put to death back then – in public.
you had to tow the line & know your place.
normal life – with severe penalties.

& this new "immortality cult"
was scary:

messing with the old gods;
messing with the meaning of death.

surely, you were just born lucky & wealthy – or you weren't?
what was this thing about *choosing* eternal life?

today, such a death would still be a damn good watch

& religion
is still a confounding, risky business.

DESCRIPTION OF A HOME

a painting with the words: I HATE ABBA. a turquoise neon light in the shape of an X. A sofa covered in bright blue & red vinyl. a drinks receipt from the Chateau Marmont Hotel in Hollywood. a *Time* magazine with a cover-story about the killing of Osama Bin Laden. a child's plastic "Baby Bop" toy which once contained shampoo. an empty tequila bottle. a flattened beer bottle cap printed with the All Black logo. a t-shirt with a warrior goddess riding on the back of a wolf. a book containing a thesis on the audio-visual poetics of *Miami Vice*. an unframed reproduction of a Picasso *Dora Maar*. a pair of pinkish-purple broken sunglasses that belonged to an ex-girlfriend. the autobiography of Marlon Brando, with a confession about his penis shrinking to the size of a peanut, during the filming of *Last Tango in Paris*. a 1970 *Playboy* magazine featuring Playmate of the Year Claudia Jennings, who later "James Deans" on the Pacific Coast Highway. a metal fork from a second-hand store in Texas.

moments from the collector's life can be seen in these objects. the collector admires these objects for what they are, but is also reminded of anchors, the sea. the collector also thinks of them as wondrous, glittering carcasses hauled & dragged from time's rotting, dismembered rooms.

DRINK UP

today, the light is good. strong, not too bright.
just the right measure to see reality: my old friend.
my bedrock, on which all my bullshit & aspirations are based.
a departure point, but also a harbour of shelter.

I've got all my favourite memories in my top pocket; a
few grains of ambition left on the shelf –
& a few stars twinkling on the horizon.
I am able to resolve all unresolved issues in my mind.

I feel at peace in this place. did I mention the heavenly
light at the bar?
(I'm served by fallen angels.)

am I giving my all to my loved ones? kids? my beer-
shitting buddies?
hey I do okay. I'm tuned in.
& as they say in showbiz, always leave them wanting more.
does the void give a fuck?

yeah, I know I gotta change… but that's another story too.
& – Jesus…
yeah, I've heard about that spiritual thing.

GREEN BLUEZ

it might be a green traffic light on a blue morning
it might be Wild Lupine in a field of Wavy Hair-grass
it might be the colour of the sea
it might be olives served on a cerulean blue platter
it might be a blue room inside a house painted green
it might be tears cried by a pounamu adze
it might be Chinook helicopters flying back into the *wild blue yonder*
it might be blues for planet Earth
it might be a metaphor for an emotional metamorphosis

the opposite of green bluez might be red orangez

BACK TO BOROBUDUR

for Penny

again
I press the stone with my feet –
others lie down on the path & kiss the sacred ground.

moving clockwise, upwards
in a lime cobalt burgundy batik smiling crowd –

a cell-phone camera-clicking parasol day,
journey thru warm massage
of air –

breathing in spiritual geometry, carved-stone stories,
statues of B. – some without heads – once stolen or given
away,

imagining guide-told secret panels
& looking out across central point Java landscape –

a time-machine mental self-assessment:
so, again – life?

the entire ninth-century monument was once lost for centuries
& is still sometimes covered by Merapi's volcanic ash!

Buddha
can be anything that falls out of the sky!

'Isn't it beautiful?' – I say to my friend.
'Too many people & not as good as a church, which
is a more practical, functional thing. I mean – no
roof!' he replies. 'You can do things inside a church.'

REFLECTION ON A CRUSH WHILE LOOKING AT THAT PHOTO OF PRESIDENT OBAMA, HILARY CLINTON, ETC, IN THE SITUATION ROOM – WATCHING & WAITING FOR NEWS OF OPERATION NEPTUNE SPEAR

all I had to go on was an awkward arrangement
to meet outside work, sometime
which never happened.

I was sure there was sex inside
her frequent auburn-hair framed stare –
&, for months, I longed to scuba dive
that aura, leap recklessly into deep water.

all I got
was reflective park-walking thru photosynthetic landscapes
with a starved green face,
a talking mirror – pondering her signals
& a slow decline into my seat at the coffee shop –
going over snatches of coded conversation.

I wanted *something* for my trouble.
often, you get what you deserve:
emotional g-forces which can fuck-up daily life
& a little bit of terror in the heart.

It was typical fallout from unrequited romantic yearning –
the sort of thing that should be taught about in school,
but never will be.

finally,
a blast of clarity & freedom came one afternoon
like a peace-bringing gunshot to the obsession,
as I vandalised a red booth seat by distractedly doodling
her name.

it was a problem that had to be put to sleep
because it had nailed me,
just as efficiently as those hard-ass Navy Seal bastards did
on that secret mission in Pakistan.

IT'S A GOOD DAY TO GO LOOKING FOR FRESH MANGO

wash face trim beard pants on breakfast eat –
step thru well-rehearsed drama of street:

broken bike
scrawny cat
oil on road
bones of rat
man taking piss – feeling relief
art on wall says *FUCK THE POLICE*
ATM down
worthless space
cigarette smoke pulls a face
orange dirt on bitumen
mosquito sticks proboscis in
blocks of ice
bowls of rice
falling leaf
grinning teeth

& Ondel-Ondel of Betawi too –
huge head wobbling
sticks of bamboo

WHEN I WAS 12

I bought a ticket at the Victory Theatre
one Saturday afternoon to see a movie about the
Red Baron.

his tri-plane is still the coolest airborne
death-machine ever made.

I watched him go about his business
with a packet of Snifters & a Choc-Bomb
for company.

kids excitedly rolled red Jaffas
under the ancient cracked vinyl seats –

little rolling balls of blood, amid the adrenaline rush:
watching the Baron rain a shit-storm of tracer upon
his targets.

I walked home with a new hero
& full of that euphoric feeling that comes

when you shoot your enemy

|

|

|

|

|

|

down

CICCIOLINA

Cicciolina is a world-famous Italian porn star
& one-time member of Parliament.

she offered to do it with Saddam Hussein
& prevent war.

Cicciolina liked going down.
Saddam just liked gassing people.

she was going to clean his pipes
but he passed.

he was a bad boy & he was going
down, anyway.

he should have said yes.
have you seen her lips?

her lips could have changed history.
let's hear it for Cicciolina:

she knew that men are truly at peace
when they've fucked their brains out.

that's how fragile men are.

Printed in Australia
AUOC02n0831250815
269826AU00010B/33/P

9 781925 231113